Mighty Mighty MONSTERS

THE MONSTER CROOKS

Raintree

www.raintreepublishers.co.uk
Visit our website to find out
more information about
Raintree books.

To order:
☎ Phone 0845 6044371
🖹 Fax +44 (0) 1865 312263
📠 Email myorders@raintreepublishers.co.uk

Customers from outside the UK please telephone +44 1865 312262

Raintree is an imprint of Capstone Global Library Limited,
a company incorporated in England and Wales having its registered
office at 7 Pilgrim Street, London, EC4V 6LB
– Registered company number: 6695582

First published by Stone Arch Books in 2010
First published in the United Kingdom in paperback in 2012
The moral rights of the proprietor have been asserted.

Edited by Siân Smith
Originated by Capstone Global Library Ltd
Printed and bound in China by South China Printing Company

ISBN 978 1 406 24228 7 (paperback)
16 15 14 13 12
10 9 8 7 6 5 4 3 2 1

British Library Cataloguing in Publication Data
O'Reilly, Sean, 1974
741.5-dc23
A full catalogue record for this book is available
from the British Library

THE MONSTER CROOKS

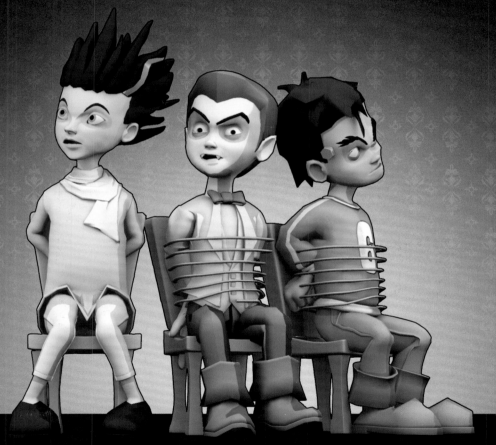

created by
Sean O'Reilly

illustrated by
Arcana Studio

In a strange corner of the world known as Transylmania . . .

Legendary monsters were born.

WELCOME TO TRANSYLMANIA

But long before their frightful fame, these classic creatures faced fears of their own.

To take on terrifying teachers and homework horrors,
they formed the most fearsome friendship on Earth . . .

Mighty Mighty MONSTERS

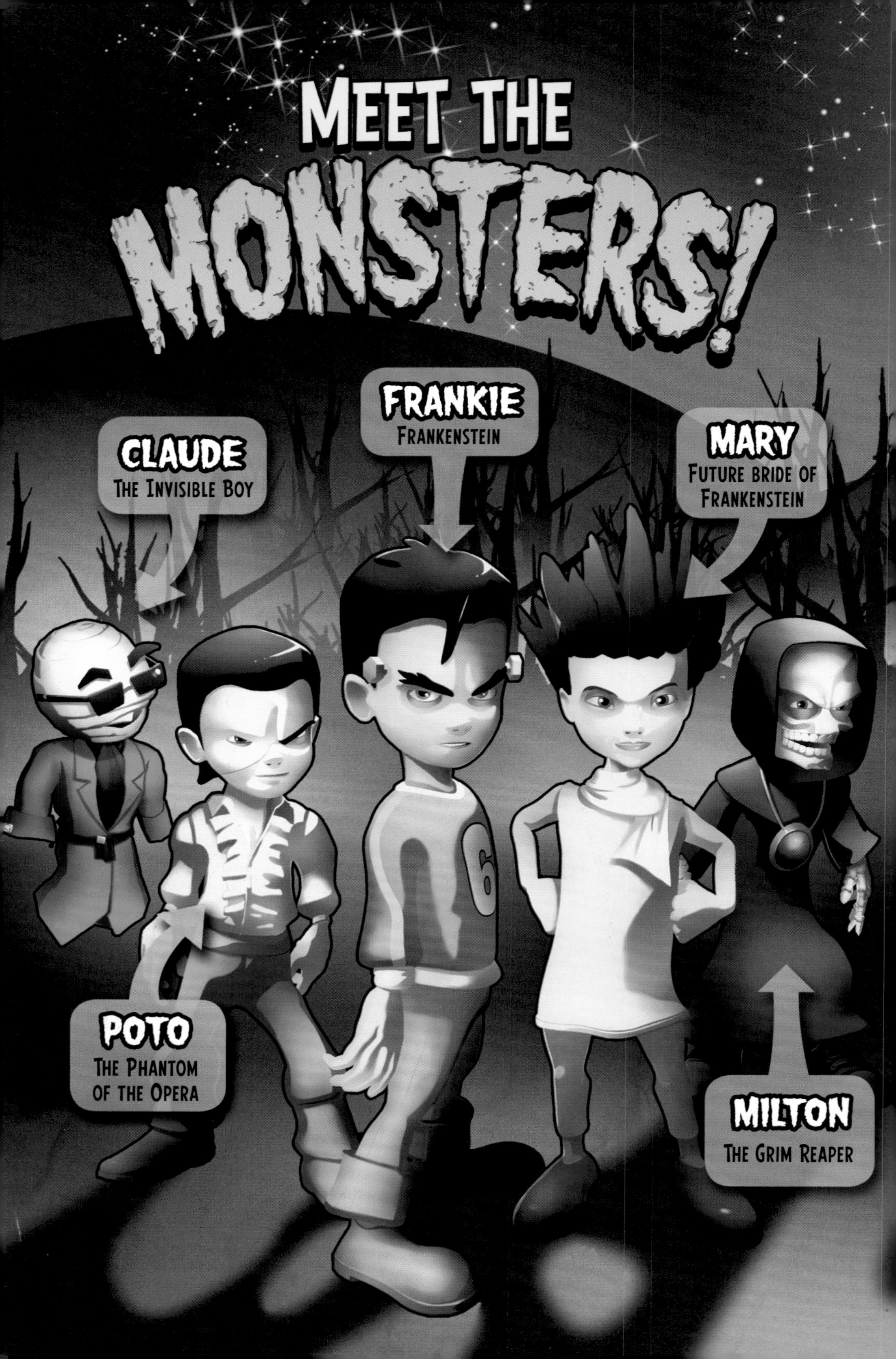
MEET THE
MONSTERS!
CLAUDE
THE INVISIBLE BOY
FRANKIE
FRANKENSTEIN
MARY
FUTURE BRIDE OF FRANKENSTEIN
POTO
THE PHANTOM OF THE OPERA
MILTON
THE GRIM REAPER

IGOR
The Hunchback

KITSUNE
The Fox Girl

TALBOT
The Wolfboy

VLAD
Dracula

WITCHITA
The Witch

At the Transylmania Youth Centre...

They've got to be in there!

This is huge! I can't wait to show them my bag!

8

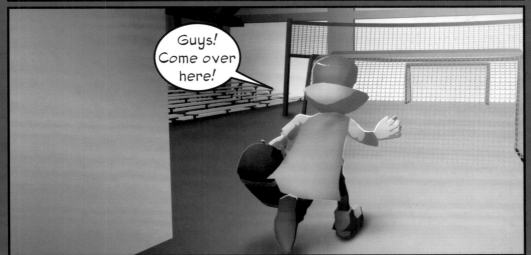

13

After spending the morning at the pool, I was on my way home.

I had my bag, with nothing in it but a wet swimsuit, a towel, and some extra clothes.

Then...

Oof!

Whoa!

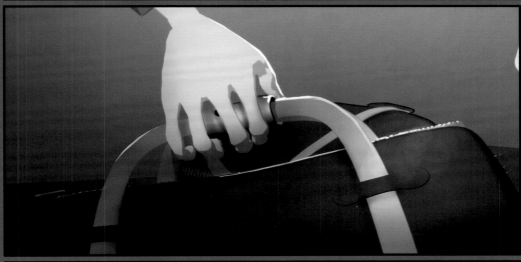

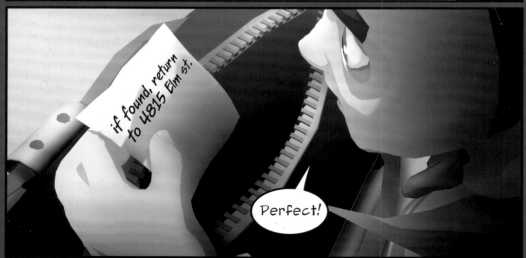

An hour later...

We can't be far now.

ELM ST.

I know we're close. This way!

Well, we're here. Now what?

Knock on the door, I guess.

KNOCK! KNOCK! KNOCK!

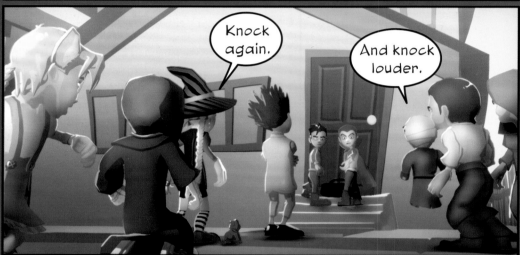

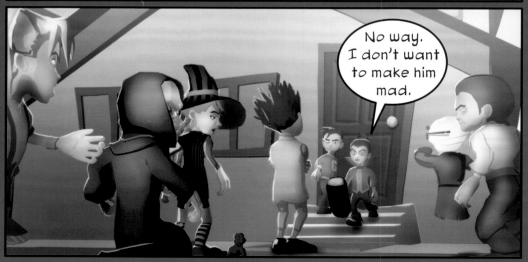

We can't just give up.

But we can't just leave the bag on the doorstep.

We could really use a bloodhound to find some clues.

Brilliant idea, Claude! I know just who to ask!

Meanwhile, Talbot was trapped at the library for summer school.

What's that noise?

Hey, Talbot! Get out here.

23

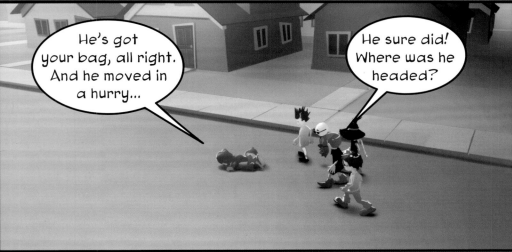

25

27

NOW!

Grrrrr! In a hurry?

Easy, boy. We ain't gonna hurt no one.

35

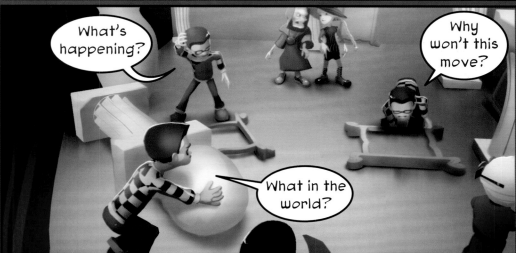

FAMOUS
ART HEISTS

—In 1911, Leonardo da Vinci's famous *Mona Lisa* painting was stolen from the Louvre museum in Paris, France. Vincenzo Peruggia stole the painting while he was working. It was found two years later.

—In 1990, the biggest art heist in US history took place at the Isabella Stewart Gardner Museum in Boston. Two men claiming to be police officers handcuffed security guards and shut off the alarm system. They took 13 pieces, which included works by Vermeer, Rembrandt, and Manet. All of the items are still missing.

—In 2003, three paintings by Van Gogh, Picasso, and Gauguin were stolen from the Whitworth Gallery in Manchester, England. The thieves avoided cameras, alarms, and guards to take the famous works. A note was left saying that the pieces were stolen to point out how bad the security was at the gallery. All three paintings were found the next day, stuffed behind a toilet at an underground station.

—In 2004, two famous Edvard Munch pieces were stolen from the Munch Museum in Oslo, Norway. Thieves with guns walked into the museum and took *The Scream* and *Madonna*. The paintings were recovered with slight damage in 2006.

GLOSSARY

adventure an exciting experience

confession a statement admitting guilt

faint not very strong

favour something helpful or kind that you do for someone

heist robbery

masterpieces outstanding pieces of work

priceless so valuable that it is not possible to put a price on it

scent a smell

thieves people who steal things

DISCUSSION QUESTIONS

1. Vlad was excited to show his friends his bag. What did you think Vlad had inside the bag before he opened it?

2. The monsters decided not to call the police. Do you think they should have? Explain your answer.

3. The monsters didn't take the reward money. Would you have taken the reward? Why or why not?

WRITING PROMPTS

1. Witchita comes up with a great spell to stop the art thieves. Write your own spell to stop the crooks.

2. Write a small article for the local newspaper about the monsters and their heroic efforts in catching the art thieves.

3. Pick your favourite monster and write a small paragraph explaining why you like him or her.

INFORMATION BOOKS

The Mystery of Vampires and Werewolves
(Can Science Solve?), Chris Oxlade (Heinemann
Library, 2008)

Scary Monsters, Jim Whiting (First Fact Books, 2010)

GRAPHIC NOVELS

Dracula (Graphic Revolve), Bram Stoker, retold by
Michael Burgan (Raintree, 2009)

Frankenstein (Graphic Revolve), Mary Shelley, retold
by Michael Burgan (Raintree, 2009)

The Monster of Lake Lobo, Scott Nickel (Stone
Arch Books, 2007)

WEBSITE

learnenglishkids.britishcouncil.org/en/make-
your-own/make-your-monster
Visit this website to create your own monster. You
can also invent your own scary story, dangerous
animal, or superhero.

Mighty Mighty MONSTERS ADVENTURES

Hide and Shriek!
ISBN: 978 1 406 23718 4

Lost in Spooky Forest
ISBN: 978 1 406 23720 7

The King of Halloween Castle
ISBN: 978 1 406 23719 1

New Monster in School
ISBN: 978 1 406 23723 8

Monster Mansion
ISBN: 978 1 406 23721 4

My Missing Monster
ISBN: 978 1 406 23722 1

Monster Beach
ISBN: 978 1 406 24226 3

The Missing Mummy
ISBN: 978 1 406 24227 0

The Monster Crooks
ISBN: 978 1 406 24228 7

The Toy Snatcher
ISBN: 978 1 406 24230 0

The Wolfboy's Wish
ISBN: 978 1 406 24231 7

The Scare Fair
ISBN: 978 1 406 24229 4

They're Fang-tastic!

ABOUT
SEAN O'REILLY
AND ARCANA STUDIO

As a lifelong comics fan, Sean O'Reilly dreamed of becoming a comic book creator. In 2004, he realized that dream by creating Arcana Studio. In one short year, O'Reilly took his studio from a one-person operation in his house to an award-winning comic book publisher with more than 150 graphic novels produced for Harper Collins, Simon & Schuster, Random House, Scholastic, and others.

Within a year, the company won many awards including the Shuster Award for Outstanding Publisher and the Moonbeam Award for top children's graphic novel. O'Reilly also won the Top 40 Under 40 award from the city of Vancouver and authored *The Clockwork Girl* for Top Graphic Novel at Book Expo America in 2009.

Currently, O'Reilly is one of the most prolific independent comic book writers in Canada. While showing no signs of slowing down in comics, he now also writes screenplays and adapts his creations for the big screen.